Original title:
Petals and Prose

Copyright © 2025 Creative Arts Management OÜ
All rights reserved.

Author: Benjamin Caldwell
ISBN HARDBACK: 978-1-80566-590-8
ISBN PAPERBACK: 978-1-80566-875-6

Stories Woven in Green

In the garden of quirks, where the daisies collide,
Silly tales twirl like the leaves in the tide.
Worms wear tiny hats, it's a sight to behold,
While the sun-baked scarecrow starts spouting bold.

Stems of Subtle Stanzas

Bees buzz like critics with sweet, sticky praise,
As flowers prance around in a color parade.
The roses gossip, oh what a bright shade,
While the tulips just laugh, their jokes never fade.

The Garden of Written Whispers

Whispers of humor dance on soft breeze,
Where laughter grows wild, snickering trees.
Ants hold a meeting to plan little jests,
While the moon winks down at their tiny requests.

Blooms Beneath the Ink

In the ink-drenched soil, puns take their root,
With rhymes growing upwards like a silly fruit.
Every line's a giggle, every verse a cheer,
As the flowers burst forth, tickling the ear.

Syllables in the Garden's Glade

In the garden where flowers dance,
A bee bumped the bud and lost its pants.
The daisies laughed, oh what a scene,
As the poor bee blushed, bright and green.

A snail in a race, oh what a sight,
Fell asleep halfway, it's quite a plight.
The tortoise mocked, 'You'll never win!'
But the race was a joke, where's the spin?

The daisies whispered, 'Let's have some fun!'
A caterpillar joined, thinking he'd run.
But he tripped on a leaf, oh what a blunder,
And the whole garden roared with laughter like thunder.

A spirited breeze joined the play, you see,
Tickling the tulips, making them flee.
With colors so loud, they jiggled around,
In the glade where joy and giggles abound.

The Luster of Leafy Legends

In the woods where the silly squirrels chatter,
They found a new nut, oh what a platter!
They wore tiny hats, feeling so grand,
Planning a feast, a bravely bold band.

A fox with a cape, thinks he's a star,
Sang to the trees, yet they seemed afar.
They shook their branches, 'Oh what a tune!'
It echoed the forest, beneath the bright moon.

A rabbit in spectacles read a fine book,
While the owl rolled its eyes, just took a quick look.
'That's how you hop? With your nose in a tale?'
But the rabbit just grinned, 'Now watch me unveil!'

The vines hung low, tickling toes,
As the sun joined in with warming glows.
In this leafy realm, laughter unwinds,
Magic in moments, where whimsy abides.

Petal to the Page

A flower thought it could write,
With ink made from morning dew.
It scribbled poems in delight,
But bees buzzed, "What's wrong with you?"

A daisy tried to take the stage,
Reciting verses oh so grand.
It fell right off, a funny gauge,
Landed squarely in the sand.

Heartbeats of the Growing Season

In spring, the flowers dance and sway,
With colors bright, they make a fuss.
They giggle as they sway away,
"Oh look, I'm bright, just like that bus!"

The sun came out, but not alone,
A cloud popped in to take a peek.
"Is this a garden or a throne?"
"I'll reign here till you're all a leak!"

The Whisper of Roots and Rhymes

The roots are whispering underground,
In jokes that only they can hear.
With rumbles, giggles all around,
"Don't poke! That tickles, oh dear!"

A worm popped up to join the jest,
"Your puns are deep, but I'm the best!"
In laughter, they became the test,
Who's the king of tiny fest?

Ferns and Feelings Intertwined

A fern had feelings – don't you scoff,
It loved a leaf, oh what a plight!
When that leaf waved, the fern took off,
Cried, "I'm rooted, but what a sight!"

The leaves giggled, and the rain just laughed,
As they spun tales of leafy glee.
In every droplet, joy was craft,
Nature's whimsy, wild and free!

Pollen and Pen

In a garden of scribbles, I fell,
Where jumbled thoughts blossom and swell.
The bees buzz with laughter, I must confess,
My pen's in a tussle, making a mess.

With each little stroke, a flower takes flight,
Spilling my secrets in pure daylight.
The daffodils giggle, the tulips they wink,
As pollen drips down from my ink.

Expressions from the Verdant Tides

The daisies debate, who wears the best hat,
While my ink spills out like a chatty old cat.
The ferns are convinced they're the life of the show,
Making wisecracks with a flair, don't you know?

Dripping with color, the violets tease,
Crafting new phrases with the greatest of ease.
The laughter erupts like a fountain's grand leap,
My paper's a garden where humor runs deep.

Bound by the Beauty of Nature

In the grip of a vine that tickles my chin,
I find inspiration, the laughs dive right in.
The sunflowers grin as they sway to the beat,
While rhymes twist and twirl in a dance so sweet.

The couch grass is plotting mischief tonight,
As fireflies sketch shadows, a puzzling sight.
With every new scribble, they giggle in glee,
Nature's a comedian, can't you see?

Harmonies of the Floral Muse

A chorus of colors in harmony sing,
Each blossom reveals such a whimsical thing.
The lilacs are laughing, the roses bemused,
As paper and petals become quite confused.

Writing out jokes with a lilting breeze,
Every word flutters, tickles like leaves.
A symphony blooms in the laughter we blend,
In nature's own garden, the fun never ends.

Verses of the Verdant Realm

In a garden where laughter blooms,
Squirrels juggle with funny brooms.
Rabbits tap dance, quite absurd,
While flowers giggle, not a word.

The bees wear shades and buzz in style,
Chasing dreams across each mile.
Worms play hide-and-seek in soil,
Cheering for their garden toil.

The sun spills rays like melted cheese,
Tickling plants with every breeze.
Frogs croak jokes with great delight,
As fireflies blink, lighting the night.

A tomato rolls, oh what a sight,
Running from the salad's bite.
In this green realm, joys unfold,
With stories shared, and laughter told.

Petal Soft Verses

Chirping birds share secret tales,
While daffodils giggle in colorful veils.
Bumblebees buzz with comic flair,
Tickling tulips, swaying in air.

A lazy bloom told a pun to a weed,
Said, 'I'm thriving, you just feed!'
While daisies dance, they swap some sass,
Chasing raindrops, oh what a class!

Under the sun, sunflowers grin,
Chasing butterflies, aiming to win.
Petunias play hide-and-seek, oh my!
As playful breezes pass by and sigh.

Laughter echoes through the green,
In this soft realm, what a scene.
Every blossom has a jest,
In this garden, joy is the best!

Canvas of the Earth

On the canvas where colors play,
A painter's brush goes wild today.
The daisies splash in hues of glee,
While orange poppies sing out, 'Whee!'

The clouds like cotton candy float,
While bees bob about on a silly boat.
Chasing sweet nectar with a twist,
In a world where joy can't be missed.

A pebble sings beneath the sun,
Tickling the ants just for fun.
While rain dances down, a splashy ride,
And mud puddles become a slide.

Colors mix and laughter spills,
As the world showcases quirky thrills.
In this vibrant mix, life's absurd,
Each stroke of joy, simply unheard.

Blossoms in the Art of Words

In the ink of laughter, stories grow,
As petals whisper what they know.
A cactus jokes, 'I'm prickly wise!'
While daisies pop up with surprise.

A willow weeps, but not with sorrow,
It's just a wiggle for tomorrow.
The daisies declare a poetry fight,
As bumblebees cheer with sheer delight.

The sun winks as the moon plays coy,
In glorious verses, oh what joy!
Roses tease with fragrant tales,
While violets hum in playful scales.

In the garden of laughter and rhyme,
Every petal knows how to chime.
In this art of jests and fun,
Each line's a rainbow; every one!

Ink and Nectar

I spilled my drink on the page, oh dear,
The characters all swam like fish in beer.
My plot got soggy, my rhyme turned to slop,
But laughter erupted, I couldn't just stop.

Inkwells and cider make quite the blend,
A liquid adventure that seems to transcend.
Characters dancing on the table's top,
In puddles of giggles, we'll never stop!

Poems of the Swirling Breeze

The wind tickles papers, they swirl and they fly,
Pages like kites, soaring up to the sky.
Words caught in whirlwinds, they tumble with glee,
Haikus on breezes are wild, just like me.

My poems took flight on a gust, 'Whoosh!' they said,
An ode to a sandwich, quite silly I dread.
I chased down my verses, they slipped out of hand,
In the chase of a rhyme, I slipped on the sand!

Colorful Narratives of the Earth

I wrote about rainbows and fields full of cheer,
But ended up writing, 'My shoe's stuck in here!'
The colors all giggled, the grass wore a frown,
As I tangled in weeds, flopped face-first to the ground.

Stories of sunshine, of daisies so bright,
Yet my tale took a twist when a bee took a bite.
I swatted and chuckled, ran in zig-zagging spree,
For nature's sharp humor is dizzying glee!

Sweet Notes in Floral Symphony

In a garden of laughter, I scribble and sing,
Each flower a note to the joy that they bring.
But daisies whisper secrets, that's where I was caught,
In a symphony of giggles, oh dear, what a plot!

Bumblebees buzzing, composing in flight,
While tulips crack jokes till they fall over, right?
With violins made of leaves, we danced for a while,
In this whimsical garden, every flower could smile!

Nature's Quill and Ink

In the garden, a mouse writes,
With a nib made of tiny bites.
He scribbles tales of cheese delight,
While the birds cackle with pure fright.

The flowers blush, each shade a jest,
As they bloom in their Sunday best.
A snail races, slow and spry,
Challenged by a butterfly who flies high.

The bees buzz gossip, oh what fun,
Swapping secrets 'til the day is done.
They dance in circles, a dizzy affair,
And the ants march in with perfect flair.

So here's to nature's silly pen,
Where laughter dances time and again.
Each line a chuckle, tears of mirth,
This is the magic of our earth!

Verses on the Wind

The wind whispers jokes to the trees,
Rustling leaves, laughing with ease.
A squirrel quips, 'I've lost my nut!'
Then plops on the ground with a hilarious 'thut!'

Clouds drift by in a soft parade,
Sharing puns while the sun does fade.
"Oh look! A sheep wearing a hat!"
"That's no sheep! It's just a cat!"

The brook babbles tales of silly fish,
Who dream of swimming in a gourmet dish.
As frogs croak out the next big scene,
A wise old turtle shrugs and leans.

Nature's laughter fills the air,
With giggles that flow everywhere.
So join the chorus, let out a cheer,
For whimsical verses are always near!

Leaves of Lyrical Light

In autumn's glow, the leaves take flight,
Dancing in a twirl, quite a sight.
A pumpkin grins, his face all carved,
While the scarecrow stands, quite starved.

The harvest moon rolls by with sass,
Synced with laughter, not a moment to pass.
A raccoon steals pies with a cheeky grin,
While the barn cat plots how to sneak in.

Comets of squirrels dart overhead,
Chasing each other, full of dread.
'The sky is ours!' they yell with glee,
But crash! A branch, their destiny.

With every rustle, stories unfold,
Of mischief and pranks, all mighty bold.
So let the leaves dance, shout, and play,
In this lyrical light, we'll join the fray!

Scented Sonnets in Spring

In spring the blooms host a grand soiree,
With daisies dressed in bright array.
The dandelions tease, 'We're here to stay!'
While tulips nod, 'We'll join the play!'

Butterflies flit with a stylish flair,
While ladybugs claim they're debonair.
"Oh, look at us! We are so fine!"
A bumblebee hums, "Well, I'm all mine!"

The raindrops dance in a syncopated beat,
As worms wiggle up for a springtime treat.
A chorus of frogs croons at the pond,
While a wise old owl chuckles and responds.

Nature's humor fills the air,
With scents and giggles, everywhere.
So put on your boots, come take a swing,
In the garden of laughter, let's joyfully sing!

Inked in Nature's Breath

In a garden where giggles bloom,
The squirrels wear hats, making room.
A cactus dances, prickly and bright,
While daisies gossip from morning till night.

A bumblebee buzzes in perfect tune,
Sipping on nectar, oh what a boon!
The flowers debate who's the fairest,
As daisies insist, it's the one who's the rarest.

A tree stands tall, with stories to tell,
Of acorns that fell and the times that they fell.
Its branches reach out, a leafy embrace,
While the sun's grinning down, a warm, golden face.

So if you find joy in this whimsical place,
Join the frolic and the nature's race.
For humor thrives where the wild things are,
And laughter showers like rain from a star.

Versed in Sunshine's Gaze

The sun peeks through with a cheeky grin,
As flowers compete where the fun begins.
A tulip wears shades, looking so fly,
While daisies form a conga, oh my!

A little worm wiggles with great flair,
Telling the butterflies, "I'm almost there!"
They giggle and flutter, all in a line,
While the ants march on, feeling just fine.

A patch of grass holds a picnic delight,
Where ants steal crumbs, oh what a sight!
The ladybugs laugh at the suns' hot dance,
While the frogs join in for a crazy prance.

Laughter rings out in nature's grand play,
Where every critter adds to the sway.
Together we find the joy in the haze,
For every day's a sunny fun craze!

The Secret Language of Leaves

A rustling whisper from a leafy tongue,
Plants share secrets, like songs that are sung.
The oak sends gossip to the shy little fern,
While the willow dances, waiting for her turn.

The maple shouts, "Hey, look at my hue!"
As the pine rolls its eyes, "That's old news, boo!"
The sycamore chuckles, plotting a prank,
While the breeze giggles, adding to the rank.

A dandelion dreams beneath the blue,
Wishing to fly like a feather, so true.
While ladybugs plot with a wink and a nudge,
In nature's realm, they won't budge!

Together they laugh, amidst all the trees,
Whispering jokes caught in the breeze.
In this leafy chatter, we find the delight,
In the secret language of flora's insight.

The Ballet of Blossoms and Lines

In a meadow where blossoms take flight,
Sunflowers twirl in a pirouette light.
With petals as skirts, they spin through the air,
While bees are the dancers, without a care.

A daisy grins wide, an opening act,
While tulips jump high, in a flower-packed tact.
They sway to the wind, a whimsical beat,
With a laugh from the roses, can't be discreet!

The violets blush as they join in the spree,
While daisies tease out their partner, the bee.
Together they prance on this vibrant stage,
In the ballet of blooms, wild and sage.

Where sprouts and shoots brush up in a whirl,
In nature's grand ballet, all stories unfurl.
For laughter and joy are the steps that entwine,
Amidst the dance of the blossoms divine!

Poetic Gardens

In a garden so lush, a bee took a dive,
It buzzed through the blooms, oh, so very alive!
With each little flower, a dance it did make,
But tripped on a petal, now there's quite the quake!

The tulips all giggled, the daisies did sway,
As the bee moaned in laughter, 'What a clumsy display!'
But nature kept smiling, with humor so bright,
In this whimsical garden, everything's light.

The Palette of Nature

A painter once sat with hues all around,
But every fresh stroke, a mistake he had found.
With splashes of color, oh what a sight,
He painted a rabbit that wobbled in fright!

The bluebirds all chirped, 'What color's that, friend?'
He mixed up his greens, they began to commend.
'Just call it surprise, a whimsical style!'
And the rabbits soon joined, with a raucous guile.

Verses Among Vines

Among twisted grapevines, where laughter's the wine,
The grapes had a meeting, all could align.
'The humans are clueless, they squish us with glee,
But we cause a ruckus, just wait, you will see!'

With every sly whisper, their plans they made bold,
To roll down the hillside, a sight to behold.
The vineyard was shaking, as grapes lost their form,
And grapes in the barrel, now plotting a storm!

Daffodils and Dialect

In a field of bright daffodils, words came to play,
'The accent's all wrong!', said one in dismay.
With foliage flapping, they started to chat,
About dialects in bloom, and where they all sat!

One bloom said with a chuckle, 'I'm a 'daffy' delight!'
With a twist of the stem, it declared with sheer might.
'The tulips are jealous, they think they're more grand,
But I'm the life of the party, just check out my stand!'

Secret Lives of Flowers

In a garden full of curious blooms,
Roses wear their perfume like costumes.
Tulips gossip in colorful hues,
While daisies dance in their Sunday shoes.

Sunflowers hold meetings, peeking at the sun,
Lilies complain of the bees having fun.
Violets plot mischief by the old oak tree,
Laughing so loud, they wake up a bee.

Hydrangeas play cards, a game of Black Jack,
Chanting, "Don't let those weeds get back!"
Pansies paint faces, a comical sight,
As morning glories giggle in delight.

But beware the night, for chaos will reign,
When all the flowers meet in the rain.
Their secret lives full of laughter and cheer,
A riotous party 'til dawn draws near.

Eloquent Springs

A dandelion dressed in a ball gown bright,
Twirling 'round on a breezy night.
Anemones wink with a cheeky smile,
While crocuses boast of their springtime style.

The nonchalant fern rolls its leafy eyes,
At tulips trying to reach for the skies.
Cacti chuckle, for they know the truth,
That all these flowers were once just old youth.

Wisteria whispers of its long, wild hair,
While daffodils debate whose looks are more rare.
A cute lilac claims the best perfume,
Making lilies sigh as they sweetly bloom.

Yet in this garden, it's all in good fun,
Each flower unique, no need to outrun.
As spring spins tales, with laughter as song,
In this realm of blooms, where all belong.

Whispers of Blooming Verses

Chrysanthemums argue who's the best poet,
While marigolds claim, "You just don't know it!"
Snapdragons snap at the ones with no pen,
As petals drop 'cause they're laughing again.

Lilies stretch out in a sun-drenched pose,
Hunting for inspiration beneath their toes.
Hydrangeas scribble while sipping on dew,
Jotting down sonnets about morning's hue.

Bee balm sings loudly, a hit for the crowd,
While orchids recite, feeling overly proud.
A sunflower jokes about standing so tall,
With a grin that declares, "I can see it all!"

Together they share their poetic spree,
In a rhyming world with no need to flee.
For in laughter and words, their essence is clear,
In whispers of verses, they've nothing to fear.

Fragments of Flora's Heart

A cactus croons a love song to the moon,
While mint teases thyme, saying, "You'll swoon!"
Petunias chime in with a melody sweet,
Winking at pansies who dance to the beat.

The rose in the corner, so smitten and shy,
Dreams of a bee that buzzes on by.
Ferns write letters with ink made from dew,
Proposing a romance, would that bee be true?

Bulbs dig deep, with hope in their eyes,
While peonies plot under velvet skies.
A baby sprout wonders if love's just a game,
In a world of wild blooms, no two are the same.

With laughter at heart, they unveil their charms,
Entwined in a garden that brings such warm arms.
In this patch of delight where affection takes flight,
Flora's fragments come together—what a sight!

Inked in Blossom's Shade

In a garden where laughter grows,
Each flower a joke, everyone knows.
Tulips giggle, daisies tease,
While bees buzz puns on a warm summer breeze.

Butterflies dance in silly delight,
Wearing their wings like silly kites.
A rose says, 'I'm thorny, it's true,'
But look at my color; what a fine hue!

Gardens plot with a wink and a grin,
Where watering cans spill secrets within.
The sun tosses rays like confetti, on trees,
And flowers exchange tales with the slight rustle of leaves.

So swing by the blooms, take a seat,
Join the laughter, it's quite a treat!
With Ink and blooms all around,
You'll leave with a smile, joyfully unbound.

Rooted in Rhyme

In soil rich with laughter's embrace,
Worms tell jokes, their wriggly grace.
The daisies roll their bright little eyes,
As roots tap dance under sunny skies.

From cheerful dandelions, jokes take flight,
Complaining of lawn mowers with all their might.
While roses tease the weeds with a sigh,
'Can't you see we're the stars of July?'

Silly shadows stretch as giggles bloom,
Frog poets croak from their mucky room.
'What rhymes with lily?' they ponder aloud,
While clouds above float by, dreamy and proud.

So stroll through the roots where the fun never ends,
And join in the chat with the leaves and their friends.
In this world of green, laughter intertwines,
Making a symphony out of kiddo designs.

Floral Paints and Poetic Hues

With brushes of laughter, we'll paint the scene,
A canvas of colors both bright and serene.
While violets crack jokes in lilting tones,
And sunflowers laugh till they wobble on stones.

A painter who doddles with tulip ink,
Squints at the flowers, then starts to think.
'Can you pose, dear daffodil? Strike a pose!'
The blooms giggle softly, striking a nose.

Marigolds mingle, chitchat in strokes,
Colorful dreams spill, alongside funny folks.
The artist just chuckles, paints with great care,
Creating a bloom-land, a whimsical fair.

So splash on the colors, let madness take flight,
In the garden of humor, 'tis pure delight.
With flowers as friends, let imagination ignite,
In this funny landscape where dreams soar bright!

Ephemeral Echoes in the Breeze

The wind whispers tales of fleeting delight,
As blossoms chuckle, keeping spirits light.
'Catch me if you can!' yells a wily petal,
Sliding down the breeze like an accidental metal.

A lilac shouts, 'I'm fragrant and proud!',
While a clever daisy joins in, loud.
'Let's play hide and seek, oh come let's frolic,
In this quirky forest, it's just so symbolic!'

The breeze carries laughter, it tumbles and twirls,
As ferns dance to rhythms made by whirls.
A sprightly dandelion makes a funny face,
And wishes upon a butterfly's grace.

So lean into the laughter, let jovial glimpses,
Take root in your heart, banish all simps.
In the garden of glee, where nature takes leave,
Be merry, be silly—just simply believe!

Sunlit Lines and Shadowed Stanzas

In the garden, words take flight,
Bumblebees laugh at lines so tight.
Sunshine spills on cheeky rhymes,
As daisies plot their runtimes.

Worms recite with wiggly cheer,
While crickets conduct a concert near.
Laughter blooms in every nook,
As flowers read from their own book.

Squirrels debate the meaning of life,
While ants share tales of silly strife.
Each leaf whispers a giggly plot,
Nature's jesters, tying the knot.

The Garden's Literary Breath

In the breeze, verses gently sway,
The tomatoes thirst for some wordplay.
Zucchinis ribbing on broccoli's plight,
While radishes blush with all their might.

Butterflies dance in a rhyming spree,
Who knew flowers could be so witty?
Plots thickened like a stew gone wrong,
With every petal singing a song.

Dandelions puff jokes in the air,
As bees bring buzz to tales laid bare.
Nature's novel unfolds with glee,
In this garden, wild and funny.

Flora's Tales Intertwined

A cactus cracked a pun so dry,
While tulips giggled, oh my, oh my!
Vines unwound their tangled yarn,
As lessons sprouted, churning charm.

Leaves deliberated on fashion trends,
While bushes plotted tricks with friends.
Garden critters joining the feast,
Every moment, a joyful beast!

Wandering weeds share gossip a'plenty,
With every chuckle, their roots get windy.
In this patchwork of laughter's weave,
Flora's tales are hard to believe.

Lush Lines and Leafy Lore

Ivy whispers secrets to the trees,
Chortling softly in the spring breeze.
Petunia plays the wise old sage,
While sunflowers boast of their stage.

Grassy prose stretches far and wide,
As creatures lounge, full of pride.
Pumpkins roll out their tall, bold tricks,
While herbs engage in clever clicks.

From the soil, stories burst with cheer,
Laughter ripples, spreading near.
In this lush world, humor's the core,
A leafy tome forever to explore.

Whispers of Bloom

In the garden where giggles sprout,
Silly seeds dance about.
Bees wear tiny hats, oh what a sight,
Buzzing jokes till the fall of night.

Sunflowers sporting shades, quite bold,
Tell tales of warmth as they unfold.
Daisies chuckle in the gentle breeze,
Waving at daisies from their sunny knees.

The roses blushed, can you believe?
Caught sharing secrets, wearing their leaves.
Tulips teeter, in their shoes of green,
Swaying with laughter, a lively scene.

Underneath the bright blue sky,
The flora whisper, and oh my!
With every petal, a giggle's shared,
In this floral rom-com, all are paired.

Ink-Stained Blossoms

With ink splatters on the page,
A daffodil dreams of a grand stage.
Wielding quills with delicate grace,
They write essays on bumblebee's race.

A pansy penned a novel, you see,
About a laughable bumblebee spree.
While violets scribble in shades of blue,
Chasing whirlwinds, oh what a view!

Chrysanthemums plot with notes and pens,
To explore far and wide with all their friends.
Creating tales of garden delight,
Ink-stained petals, oh what a sight!

Each story's a blossom, fragrant and bright,
Ink-stained blooms basking in light.
In prose they flourish, with humor unfurled,
Scripting the best tales in the floral world.

Fragrant Verses

In the meadow where scents collide,
Jasmine jokes with the garlic tide.
Lavender laughs as it spritzes the air,
While the marigold plans its underwear.

Rosemary recites with a twist and a twirl,
Puns that could make even thorns whirl.
Thyme stretches songs in notes so sweet,
While tulips beatbox to a funky beat.

Sage scribbles rhymes on a buttery leaf,
Creating a tale of humorous grief.
With every whiff, a giggle's born,
Like a flower child dancing at dawn.

Amidst fragrant verses, laughter's the crown,
In this riotous garden, no one frowns.
Buds bloom with joy, the world's their stage,
In the dance of scents, they set the page.

The Language of Flowers

In a wild chat, blooms take to speech,
Silly jokes, they happily preach.
Hyacinths tell tales of their fussy fate,
While daisies debate who's truly first rate.

Orchids prance, with an elegant flair,
Winking at roses with a toss of their hair.
Laughter erupts when the daffodils croon,
Singing ballads under the bright, cheerful moon.

They whisper behind leaves, secrets in bloom,
Crafting laughter within nature's room.
Faces aglow, hearts filled with glee,
Each budding joke blooms joyfully free.

So let's gather round in this floral sphere,
For humor in gardens is always sincere.
In the language of blooms, we find pure delight,
A comedy show, in the day and the night.

Whimsy in the Meadow's Verse

In the meadow, daisies twirl,
Bees chase butterflies, what a whirl!
A rabbit wearing tiny shoes,
Dances freely, with no clues.

Grass blades tickle those who roam,
While frogs provide a ribbit poem.
Squirrels debating what's for tea,
Betting acorns, oh don't leave me!

Dandelions puffing jokes too loud,
As the wind laughs, gathering a crowd.
The clouds giggle, float on by,
Sending raindrops with a wink and sigh.

Each bloom wears a hat of cheer,
Telling secrets we hold dear.
In this place where quirks collide,
Even the sunbeam can't hide its pride.

Blooms that Speak in Silence

Roses whisper, 'We're quite shy',
Lilies sigh and wonder why.
Tulips argue over who's best,
While sunflowers boast of their quest.

In the garden, no one can hear,
The antics of the petals near.
Carnations cracking a sly joke,
As violets giggle, 'What a bloke!'

Chrysanthemums roll their eyes and wait,
'Did you hear that? It's quite late!'
Birds perched high on branches sing,
Yet the flowers are the real bling.

The silence wraps around like a shawl,
In this dance, we humor us all.
Each bloom with a story, a grin,
In a world where silliness begins.

The Alchemy of Color and Word

A bluebell spoke with tones of glee,
'Let's paint the world, just you and me!'
Roses chimed in with a flourish bright,
'We'll create a rainbow, what a sight!'

The violets plotted, 'Let's change our hue,
To shades of purple, or maybe blue.'
Daisies chimed in with witty clap,
'Colors of chaos? Now that's a wrap!'

Pansies giggled, 'What's in a name?
Let's steal the show and take the fame!'
As petals danced and colors swirled,
They crafted joy to share with the world.

With laughter echoing through the breeze,
Every bloom became a wizard with ease.
Mixing colors and words so grand,
In this garden, magic is always at hand.

Garden of Metaphors

In this garden, words grow wild,
Syntax playing, a cheeky child.
Nouns like rabbits hop with glee,
While verbs are swaying, carefree.

Similes whiffle with frantic grace,
While metaphors dress up for a race.
Adjectives giggle, peek-a-boo,
Throwing sparkles in morning dew.

Punctuation does a jig in place,
Exclamation points quicken the pace.
Commas relax, with hands on their hips,
While sentences form in rooftop slips.

The sunrise colors them all anew,
Each line blossoms, a different hue.
In this patch where thoughts intertwine,
Every concept laughs, and it's quite divine.

Tapestry of Blossoming Thoughts

In the garden of silly faces,
A sunflower dances in funny places.
With bees that hum a jazzy tune,
And frogs that croak beneath the moon.

Petunias gossip in cheeky hues,
While daisies giggle, sharing news.
The roses sneer at their own smell,
As tulips chuckle—oh, what the hell!

Petal Soft Narratives

A daffodil dreams of being a star,
Swaying shyly from afar.
With petals like skirts in colors bright,
It teases the breeze with sheer delight.

The violets whisper their secrets low,
To each passing ant that puts on a show.
While daisies pull pranks, giggling loud,
In this floral town, they're all quite proud.

Tales from the Flowerbed

In a patch of dreams, a dandelion laughed,
Telling tall tales of the winds it has waft.
It told of its travels, how it flew so high,
And all the odd things it met in the sky.

A ladybug sighed, with grace to bestow,
It painted the bugs and their tales in a row.
With beetles in jackets, so dapper and neat,
Each one a character, quite hard to beat!

Rhythms of Nature's Embrace

A bumblebee hums with a comical flair,
While squirrels dance, without a care.
A ladybird twirls in polka dot shoes,
As blossoms join in, sharing their views.

The wind starts to giggle, tickling the leaves,
While mischievous rabbits play tricks, oh, please!
In this joyful ballet, they all take their place,
Culminating laughter in nature's warm embrace.

The Language of Blossoms

In the garden, flowers chatter,
Debating who smells better.
Tulips boast, daisies snicker,
Roses claim they're always slicker.

Bumblebees serve as the judge,
Buzzing loudly, they won't budge.
Pansies giggle, violets wink,
"Who needs words? Just stop and think!"

Sunflowers stand tall and proud,
While marigolds laugh out loud.
"Hey, did you hear that daffodil?
She's all dressed up for a thrill!"

Buds gossip when no one sees,
Chasing petals in the breeze.
In this garden of silly dreams,
Laughter's woven through their themes.

Echoes of Garden Stories

Once a weed claimed it was wise,
With a quirky twist of lies.
"I've seen the world from the ground,"
The snickering crew gathered 'round.

A sunflower chimed in with glee,
"I'd share my secrets, wait and see!"
But every tale took a twist,
Leaving flowers in a mist.

Lettuce leaf turned bright like lime,
And said, "My garden's worth a rhyme!"
With every story, laughs would grow,
As breezes carried jokes to and fro.

But the gardener stepped in with a grin,
"Enough of tales, let's dig in!"
So stories turned to salad greens,
And laughter bloomed in unexpected scenes.

Stanzas Under the Sun

Beneath the sun, they stretch and sway,
Singing tunes to greet the day.
The daisies danced a waltz so swell,
"Watch out, sunflower, you'll trip and fell!"

A rose declared, "I'm the fairest here!"
With petals flapping, full of cheer.
"Let's write a poem, a dandy verse,
But keep it light, or it'll be a curse!"

Butterflies joined the festive scene,
Flitting about with kites of green.
Chasing each other, giggles galore,
In this sunlit garden, fun's in store!

But soon the shadows stretched, oh no!
"Don't worry, friends, just take it slow."
A squirrel chuckled, "The sun will stay,
Let's write more stanzas, hip-hip-hooray!"

The Color of Written Dreams

In ink of green, the dreams unfold,
Brush strokes dancing, bold and bold.
A daffodil wrote of rainy days,
While clover whispered, "This is a craze!"

"Oh look!" the zinnias start to glow,
"Let's spin our tales with colors to show!"
Petals paint their stories bright,
While bees join in, taking flight.

Chrysanthemums grumbled, "Where's the plot?"
But tulips laughed, "We've got a lot!"
"Just sprinkle some words on fragrant scents,
And let's see who's the best at events!"

Crayons melted under the sun's embrace,
Colors mingled in a wild race.
With every stroke, laughter was found,
In a garden where dreams spun 'round.

The Melody of Growth

In the garden, seeds do dance,
Wiggling wildly, take a chance.
Sprouts are giggling, can you hear?
Laughing blossoms, full of cheer.

Bumblebees buzz, a playful tune,
Swapping stories 'neath the moon.
Grumpy weeds just roll their eyes,
While flowers burst in joyful cries.

Inked in Nature's Embrace

A flower blooms with doodled flair,
Sketching sunshine in the air.
Leaves are scribbles, all around,
Nature's art is quite profound.

Insects sketch with tiny feet,
Making trails, oh so sweet!
Dandelions puff out tales,
While raindrops spill like funny fails.

Verses and Violets

Violets sing, they rhyme and sway,
Bowing low, they steal the day.
With petals bright, they tease the sun,
In this garden, all have fun.

Witty rabbits hop in glee,
Chasing shadows, wild and free.
Squirrels plot with crafty schemes,
Making mischief in their dreams.

Chronicles of the Floral Realm

Once upon a time in green,
Flowers plotted, quite the scene.
Roses grinned with cheeky flair,
Telling tales without a care.

Thorns were knights in shining guise,
While daisies laughed at silly lies.
The sun rolled by, a jovial king,
And all the blooms began to sing.

The Art of Petal Stories

In a garden where daisies just lie,
A tulip once tried to fly high.
It flapped with great flair, put on quite a show,
But alas! Down it plopped, with a soft little 'Oh!'

Then came the roses, all dressed in red,
Telling tall tales of what they had said.
'We saw it all wild, oh what a thrill!'
But the daisies just giggled, and grew very still.

A daffodil danced with a caterpillar guest,
Claiming its moves were simply the best.
But the bug just rolled, in fits of pure glee,
Said, 'Stick to the sun, my friend, just let me be!'

So they laughed in the light, as bees buzzed along,
In a world full of blooms, where stories belong.
A petal's adventure, full of humor and flair,
Who knew that such blooms had stories to share?

Essays of Elegance

In the shade of a tree sat a wise old fern,
Writing deep essays with twists and a turn.
It pondered on life, while sipping its dew,
Making notes on the wonders of growth that it knew.

A ladybug chimed in, with a laugh and a grin,
'You wrote about sunshine? Well, that's a win!'
'But how's your prose about clouds, my dear?
Your academic flair seems a bit unclear!'

Challenged, the fern took a moment to pause,
It scribbled furiously, but with no cause.
'Perhaps I should write about weeds after all,
They may lack elegance, but they still stand tall!'

In the end, they shared jokes on their leafy delight,
Arguing humor could conquer the fright.
An essay of laughter, so bright and so grand,
In the garden of wisdom, together they stand.

Blooming Narratives

A sunflower dreamed of a best-seller book,
With tales of the sun and a radiant look.
It typed late at night, by the moon's golden glow,
But with all those bright thoughts, it ran out of flow.

A bumblebee buzzed, offered help with a grin,
'The tale of your life needs a sweet little spin!
What if you add a twist about shade?
A spin on your petals, dear friend, don't be afraid!'

So they plotted and planned a whimsical tale,
With blossoms the stars, and a snail on a trail.
Of blossoms and blooms, how they thrive in the light,
And gooey, green stems that stretch out at night.

By morning they laughed at the stories they'd spun,
Narratives blooming, just bursting with fun.
They tucked all their plots in the softest of beds,
Promising adventures live on in their heads.

Leaves of Expression

Amongst the foliage, a leaf came alive,
Claiming it was destined to thrive.
It wanted to express all the sights it had seen,
From raindrops to sunbeams, to moments so keen.

A squirrel nearby, with a twitch of the tail,
Said, 'Keep it light, or you'll end up pale!'
So the leaf took a breath, and let out a chuckle,
'This journey is grand, filled with giggles and muckle!'

From critters at play, to skies full of cheer,
It noted how laughter can chase off the fear.
The wise old oak watched with a grin so wide,
As the leaf spun its yarns, full of playful pride.

So here's to the leaves, with their stories so bold,
Finding humor in life, more precious than gold.
With every swift breeze, a new tale they share,
In the heart of the forest, there's laughter to spare.

Blossom and Quill

In a garden where scribbles grow,
A bee tried to write, but stung his toe.
The flowers laughed, their colors bright,
As words took flight in sheer delight.

With daisies in hats, they danced around,
Each petal a phrase, a whimsical sound.
A sunflower shouted, 'What a great pun!'
As a butterfly wiggled, 'Oh, this is fun!'

A gardener tripped, a trowel in hand,
And stumbled upon tall tales so grand.
The tulips giggled, 'He's writing a mess!'
'But we love it still,' said the witty caress.

So come take a stroll, let laughter bloom,
An orchard of words, brightening the gloom.
In this quirky plot, friendships conspire,
With quills and blossoms, let fun never tire.

Scented Stanzas

In a patch of rhymes, where scents collide,
Rosemary jokes with lavender slides.
They chuckle and twirl, with thyme on the side,
Creating a feast of words far and wide.

Chives gave a wink, with a scent so bold,
'Oh garlic, my friend, you're a sight to behold!'
With each whimsical line, their laughter unfurls,
Mints dance about, tossing lavender pearls.

The daisies declare, 'Let's rhyme and recline,'
As a skunk cabbage moans, 'I'm feeling divine!'
With verses that tickle, and fragrances sweet,
They craft clever lines, oh what a treat!

So gather your herbs, let's write on the breeze,
A banquet of humor, guaranteed to please.
In this scented garden, your smile we'll seize,
With stanzas that chirp, and laughter with ease.

Garden of Words

In a garden of thoughts, the blooms run wild,
Each blossom a line, like a chatty child.
The roses are gossiping, oh what a spree,
'Did you see the tulips? They're wearing the key!'

A daffodil joked, 'I can't find my stem!'
While the pansies smiled, 'Let's play a gem!'
The marigolds stamped, in a quirky parade,
With laughter and puns that never would fade.

'Oh, did you hear? The violets sing!'
They giggle with glee, and a joy they bring.
'Our petal-penned dreams float up to the sky,'
As a dandelion whispered, "Give whimsy a try!"

So come, take a seat, in our wordy domain,
Where laughter grows loud, like a soft summer rain.
In this garden of humor, we dance and we play,
With verses to tickle, come join us today!

Floral Sonnet

Upon the table, blooms sit in a row,
A daisy declared, 'Let's put on a show!'
The violets giggled, with bows in their hair,
As they planned out the scenes with whimsical flair.

A clumsy old bee buzzed in with a grin,
Tripped over a petal and fell with a spin.
The flowers erupted in laughter so sweet,
'Our tale's getting better, oh what a feat!'

The sun shone bright, casting rays all around,
While the peonies rumoured, 'It's dreamland we've found!'
With a chorus of chuckles, they murmured a tune,
Creating a sonnet that danced by the moon.

So join in the fun, and let verses sway,
With giggles and puns, we'll brighten the day.
In this floral performance, we'll laugh till we drop,
As our sonnet of blooms brings joy that won't stop!

Rhymes in the Wind

A flower sneezed, gave me a fright,
As bees buzzed loudly, day and night.
I laughed so hard, my sides did ache,
I thought, what a mess, oh what a mistake!

Dandelions danced with glee,
Chasing each other, so wild and free.
A tulip winked, oh what a sight,
I'm not sure which took off in flight!

The roses gossip, oh what a tale,
They claim the daisies are really quite pale.
Every bud has a quirk to show,
Even weeds have stories, don't you know?

So here I sit, with laughter anew,
Among the blooms and skies so blue.
With rhymes that tickle and joys that spin,
Who knew the garden could make me grin?

Harvesting Metaphors

In the garden of words, I planted a seed,
Watered it daily, gave it some feed.
It grew into puns, oh what a sight,
With chuckles and giggles, sheer delight!

I gathered each phrase like ripe, juicy fruit,
Some sour, some sweet—what a hoot!
The metaphors danced in the breeze,
Tickling my mind, oh if you please!

Kaleidoscope laughter in every turn,
Words like herbs, some crisp, some stern.
Each line I picked, a jest or a quip,
I couldn't stop, oh what a trip!

So here's to the harvest, both funny and bright,
A plot full of play, in morning light.
With cautious wit and a chuckle to share,
Who knew that fiction could float in air?

A Symphony of Buds

Little buds whisper, a tune so sweet,
They sway with laughter, skipping their feet.
A symphony blooms in the morning air,
Where every petal plays, without a care.

The daisies giggle in bright yellow dress,
While violets tap dance, quite hard to impress.
A crow croaks loudly, thinks he can sing,
But flowers just laugh; he's no blooming thing!

Pansies applaud with their colorful cheer,
But roses roll eyes; oh dear, oh dear!
A chopstick flies past, is it dinner or fun?
When petals unite, the chaos has begun!

So let's join the melody, come waltz on the green,
In this garden of laughter, it's quite the scene.
With buds all around, a joke in each hue,
A symphony of smiles, forever anew.

The Written Garden

In the garden of letters, I sowed my dreams,
Each line a flower, or so it seems.
With ink as the soil, I sprinkled the quirks,
Hoping for giggles from funny little perks.

Oh look, a comma, it's doing a jig,
While exclamation marks do the boogie so big!
The nouns are all bouncing, the verbs take a dive,
In this written wonderland, words come alive!

Adjectives twirl, in their frilliest ballet,
As metaphors skip down the sunny pathway.
The garden's a canvas, with letters that play,
And every bloom whispers, "Hey, what's the say?"

So if you're feeling blue, come take a stroll,
Through the fields of fiction, let laughter console.
In the written garden, where silliness reigns,
Every paragraph tickles, in joy that remains.

Flowing Lines of Earthly Delights

In gardens where the daisies dance,
A snail once wore a shiny pants.
He slipped and slid, oh what a sight,
Decided then to take a flight.

A bee buzzed by, quite in a rush,
He stole the blooms in a crazy hush.
But flowers giggled, swayed and waved,
In their bright colors, mischief braved.

The earthworms wiggled, having fun,
Playing leapfrog under the sun.
With mud on faces, they'd cheer and moan,
"Who knew the garden's our live zone!"

So come and laugh, let joy ignite,
In nature's blooms, humor takes flight.
For all the creatures, big and small,
In this grand garden, there's room for all.

The Chorus of Nature's Poetry

The crickets hold a concert bright,
Under the stars, full of delight.
They chirp in sync, a funny tune,
While fireflies dance under the moon.

The frogs joined in with a big loud croak,
A silly joke or perhaps a poke.
While flowers nod, their faces grand,
"Let's all compose a flower band!"

The breeze plays soft on leaves so green,
Creating sounds, a lovely scene.
As laughter rings from bush to tree,
Nature's chuckles are wild and free.

So skip along these joyful trails,
Where laughter and nature never fail.
For in this chorus, light and free,
Fun grows wild as a dancing bee.

Words in Petal Form

If flowers could talk, they'd love to share,
The funniest secrets, beyond compare.
Roses would giggle about their thorns,
"Why not wear them like fancy adorns?"

Tulips would snicker, their colors so bright,
"Who wore it best? Let's have a fight!"
Daisies argue who's truly a star,
With petals for points, they'd raise the bar.

Lilies would waltz in a graceful line,
Arguing if they could outshine.
While sunflowers, tall, would boast with glee,
"Look at us! We're the tallest, you see?"

So gather round, let's hear their tales,
Of laughter and fun that never pales.
For in this garden, words flow free,
With petals gossiping joyfully.

The Weaving of Floral Dreams

In a meadow where dreams entwine,
Floral threads twirl in a line.
With laughter looped in every seam,
They craft a world, so bright, it beams.

A dandelion wished to fly,
With fluffy wishes that soar high.
He tickled bees, who buzzed around,
As laughter spread from ground to ground.

Petunias chatted in colors bold,
Telling stories not yet told.
While sunbeams played hide and seek,
In every petal, joy would peek.

So let's all weave our silly schemes,
In this garden of splendid dreams.
For every flower, in laughter beams,
In the tapestry of life, it gleams.

Dappled Light on Written Pages

In the sunlit glade, words dance and sway,
A squirrel reads lines as birds sing away.
With each little hiccup and comedic jest,
A giggling rabbit joins in for a fest.

The book takes a leap, straight up in surprise,
While the butterflies plot with a glint in their eyes.
They flutter and tumble, oh what a scene,
As the pages get tickled, they burst at the seam.

A mouse with a coffee, well, that's quite a sight,
He scribbles his tales with glee and delight.
As the shadows retreat from their whimsical play,
The laughter of paper dances through the day.

And as the sun sets, with a yawn from the trees,
All the critters gather, with laughter to tease.
For words in the dappled light can be funny,
And pages are never just dry, dull, or sunny.

Whispers of Backyard Myths

The gnomes in the garden are plotting tonight,
With tales of adventure, oh what a sight!
They tell of brave frogs who once flew with the crows,
And of trees that tap-dance in fanciful flows.

A wise old cat claims he once stole the moon,
While two squirrels debate the best nuts, like a tune.
They argue and quibble over who wears the crown,
While ants take a bet on who'll tumble down.

The flowers are gossiping, fueling the fun,
Saying snails make the best racers when both of them run.

But watch your step gently, for the worms are in charge,
They'll trip you quite slyly, their antics so large!

As shadows grow long and the stars start to peek,
All gather 'round whispers, so fable and cheek.
In this vibrant backyard, myths bloom like the dawn,
Where laughter and tales carry on and on.

Threads of Nature's Tapestry

In the fabric of green, the critters do weave,
A tapestry silly, with tricks up their sleeve.
A hedgehog in sunglasses, a spider with flair,
Dance on their threads, without worry or care.

The flowers all giggle, in colors so bright,
Changing hues, like chameleons in flight.
They whisper to daisies, 'Come join our parade!'
As the ants take center stage, balancing trade.

The breeze starts a chuckle, tickling the leaves,
While a tree full of squirrels dons outrageous sleeves.
A raccoon with a donut, oh what a delight!
In the threads of their laughs, every moment's just right.

As dusk paints the scene with a palette of fun,
The tapestry dances, the day's nearly done.
With threads spun of giggles and memories dear,
Nature's own quilt holds us all near.

Ephemeral Ink upon the Earth

Droplets of laughter, like raindrops on stone,
Create little stories that feel like homegrown.
A wise old owl laughs, with wisdom to share,
While the plants take a bow, pretending they care.

The puddles reflect, with splashes of cheer,
Where frogs put on shows, completely sincere.
They leap and they croak, in rhythmic delight,
Turning raindrops to giggles as day turns to night.

A wily old fox jots notes in the dirt,
Sketches of dreams, sprinkled 'round, not a hurt.
As the sun sips the ink with a wink at the sky,
Each moment is fleeting, yet laughter's nearby.

So let's take a stroll, through wild laughter's glide,
Where ink flows like rivers, bright colors collide.
For in this short life, with joy we will play,
Ephemeral whispers will always stay.

www.ingramcontent.com/pod-product-compliance
Lightning Source LLC
Chambersburg PA
CBHW071835160426
43209CB00003B/306